START-UP▲
UKULELE
It's never been easier to start playing ukulele!

Published by
Wise Publications
14-15 Berners Street, London W1T 3LJ, UK.

Exclusive Distributors:
Music Sales Limited
Distribution Centre, Newmarket Road, Bury St Edmunds, Suffolk IP33 3YB, UK.
Music Sales Pty Limited
20 Resolution Drive, Caringbah, NSW 2229, Australia.

Order No. AM1002991
ISBN: 978-1-84938-989-1
This book © Copyright 2011 Wise Publications, a division of Music Sales Limited.

Written and produced by David Harrison for Shedwork.
Design by Fresh Lemon.
Photography by Matthew Ward and Olivia McGilchrist.
Models: Matt Gaydon, Sarah Hopkins, David Harrison,
Maree Narelle and Stephen Sproat.
Edited by Tom Farncombe.
Printed in the EU.

With thanks to the City Lit, London.

www.musicsales.com

WISE PUBLICATIONS
part of The Music Sales Group
London / New York / Paris / Sydney / Copenhagen / Berlin / Madrid / Hong Kong / Tokyo

The ukulele has enjoyed a massive resurgence in popularity recently, becoming the instrument of choice for singers, for the classroom and for anyone learning an instrument for the first time. Its easy-to-learn, easy-to-play reputation is fully deserved, but it has many other advantages over some more mainstream instruments too: it is inexpensive, it's portable, it's versatile and it's extremely easy to care for.

Oh, and the uke sounds great too! In fact it's infectious—once people hear you playing, they'll want to have a go too.

You can get together with friends and teach them the basics in a few minutes, so you can be playing together in no time.

All in all, you can't go far wrong with the ukulele once you get a few of the fundamentals out of the way. So let's take a look at the first steps, and you'll soon be able to play lots of songs in different styles.

CHOOSING A UKULELE

As with everything, you get what you pay for. You can pick up a uke for a handful of change, but there's no guarantee it'll do the job. The most basic mass-produced instruments often lack the final care and finishing that a proper musical instrument needs, and they simply don't sound very good, so don't be tempted to go for the cheapest option. For only a little more outlay, you'll be able to buy a uke that plays well, with a musical sound.

For starters, you'll want a standard, or soprano ukulele. The concert uke, which is a couple of inches longer, will also be fine, but avoid the larger tenor and baritone types.

The soprano model is by far the most common and has the brightest sound. It's also the smallest, which makes it perfect for smaller fingers or those not used to the sort of finger stretches routinely required of guitarists.

Take a visit to a specialist music store—you might even find one that only sells ukes—and, if possible, take a musical friend with you. Have the shop assistant or your friend strum a little on the various ukes you're looking at. You'll be surprised how different they can sound.

There's no right or wrong about the way a ukulele sounds. As long as it's well-made, it's within your budget and you like the look of it, the sound is a matter of personal preference. Ideally, you should hear a few ukes with your eyes closed, so you can be led by the sound alone.

Take your time—you and your uke are going to be spending a lot of time together!

PARTS OF THE UKULELE

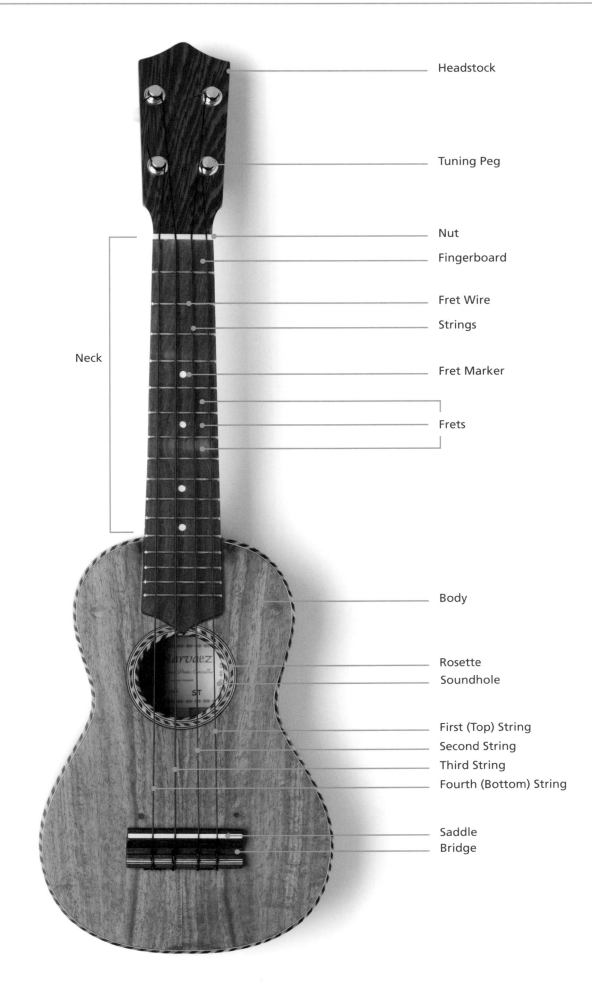

Headstock

Tuning Peg

Nut

Fingerboard

Fret Wire

Strings

Neck

Fret Marker

Frets

Body

Rosette

Soundhole

First (Top) String

Second String

Third String

Fourth (Bottom) String

Saddle

Bridge

GETTING STARTED

Once you've got your uke, there are a couple of things to sort out: first of all, you'll need somewhere to practise.

In the next section, we'll look at ways to hold the ukulele, but if you choose to sit, make sure you find a seat that allows you to keep a straight back and place your feet firmly on the floor; or a stool with a foot rail to support your feet.

Frankly, you won't need much more than the ukulele to begin playing, but there are a few accessories that might make life a bit easier.

Firstly, an electronic tuner: these are cheap and easy to use, and very accurate. Some clip on to your ukulele, and others can be put on a desk in front of you.

A music stand is another useful addition: it allows you to place your music at eye-level, and this will help to keep a comfortable posture. The height can be adjusted to let you stand or sit, as you prefer, and most stands come with little arms that will hold your songbook open at the right page.

You could also invest in a stand to keep your uke safe and prevent it from being knocked over. If you're intending to take your ukulele out and about you might like to consider a hard case that offers excellent protection—otherwise, a padded soft case will probably be sufficient.

A spare set of strings is a good idea, although you're unlikely to break them with normal wear. With proper technique and care, a set of strings will last a good long while.

Finally, it's worth keeping a nail file handly—you'll find that it's invaluable for keeping your fingernails in shape on both hands.

TOP TIP

If the tuning pegs on your uke are the type held in place with a small screw underneath, spend a moment ensuring that they're finger-tight: it'll help prevent them from slipping out of tune.

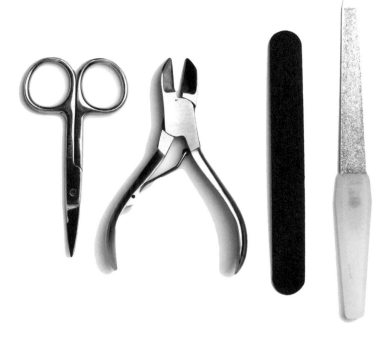

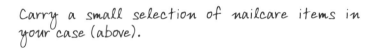

Clip-on style tuners are especially convenient (see the section on electronic tuners on page 11).

Carry a small selection of nailcare items in your case (above).

A solid case (below) offers good protection and a handy place to store spare strings, a tuner and your music too.

It's worth keeping a spare set of strings (below). Let your local music store show you how to install them on your uke.

HOLDING THE UKULELE

A good posture leads to good technique, so it's worth taking a moment to make sure you're holding the ukulele correctly and—above all—comfortably. Be sure to keep a straight back and relaxed shoulders.

Having your books on a music stand means that you'll be able to look straight ahead, and there'll be no need to hunch or stoop.

Whether standing or sitting, hand position is especially important, so let's take a look at the basics.

STANDING

If you're standing, adopt an upright, balanced stance, with both feet firmly on the floor and shoulders straight. Support the uke by gently clasping it against your body. The right forearm holds the uke at about the bottom of the ribcage, against the right side of the stomach, as shown. The uke should stay in place without the need for the left arm. Experiment until the uke remains in position.

SITTING

If you decide to sit, the technique is similar. As mentioned previously, choose a seat that lets you keep a good upright posture. Ideally, the right forearm should continue to hold the uke in position, but in practice you might let the lap take a little of the weight as long as you don't let the position of the instrument 'sag' too much. As with the standing position, the left hand shouldn't need to take any of the weight.

LEFT-HAND POSITION

Whether standing or sitting, the left hand is there to fret the strings, and not to support the neck. Place the thumb around the back of the neck at the headstock end, as shown, without pressing or gripping. When you place the fingertips on the strings, it should take very little effort, and as long as you remember to clasp the uke with the right forearm, the left hand will be free to focus on fretting the strings.

If you're holding the uke correctly, you will be looking right down onto the side of it, and it won't be very easy to see what's happening at the front. Initially, you might like to try playing in front of a mirror to make sure you're maintaining a good stance. A mirror can also help you keep track of what the left fingers are doing without having to look down at the fingerboard continually.

Make sure your body is relaxed, so you don't develop strains. If you feel any part of you getting sore, take a little rest and have a look to see whether you can change anything about the way you're holding the ukulele that will help.

TUNING

Getting the ukulele in tune is a crucial skill. There are various methods, but they all involve adjusting the pitch of the open (unfretted) strings by turning the tuning pegs to tighten or loosen each string until it sounds the correct note. Let's look at the main methods.

Start with the string nearest you and tune them one at a time. The uke is unusual among stringed instruments in that the strings are not arranged in order of pitch. Technically known as a *re-entrant* tuning, the two outer strings are tuned higher than the middle ones.

Let's look at the sound source method first. Below are the notes you need on the piano and the appropriate strings on the ukulele. The lowest-sounding string is tuned to the note known as *middle C*.

You can choose a sound source to tune against, such as a piano, pitch pipes, special audio tracks or a tuning fork; or else you can use an electronic tuner, which will tell you when your ukulele is in tune.

Eventually, your ears will tell you when one of the strings slips out of tune, and you'll find yourself tweaking the tuning pegs almost without having to think about it.

> Conventionally the G string is known as the bottom string, with the A known as the top string—this comes from instruments on which the strings are in order of pitch, such as the guitar, mandolin and violin. These terms are not quite so meaningful on the uke but, as we'll see when we look at tablature, they still have their uses.

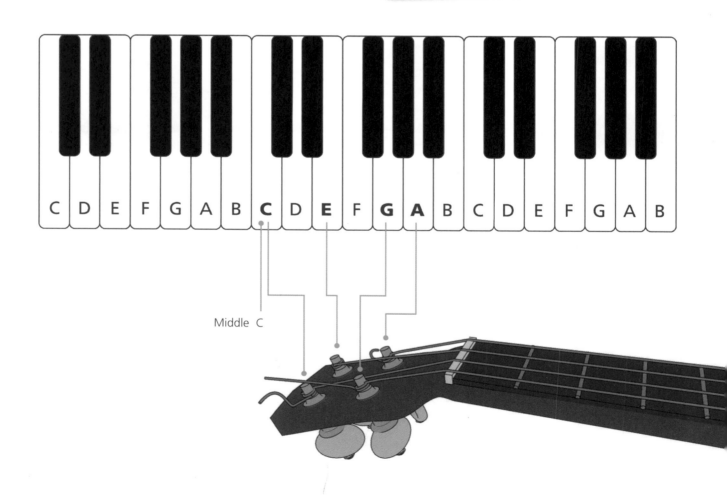

Middle C

Relative Tuning

If you tune the C string accurately, you can then use that string to tune the others.

Here's how it works:

- Place a finger on the 7th fret of the C string—this will give you the note you need (G) to tune the open fourth string (also known as the *bottom* string).

- Once that's done, play a note on the 4th fret of C string. It'll be E, which is the note you need for the open second string.

- Finally, play a note on the 2nd fret of the fourth string to sound A, which is the note you'll need to tune the first string (the *top* string).

Although it might seem a bit fiddly, this method is great for checking a single string if you're in the middle of playing, and since it relies on your ears it's great training too... check the diagram below for fret positions for each of the reference notes.

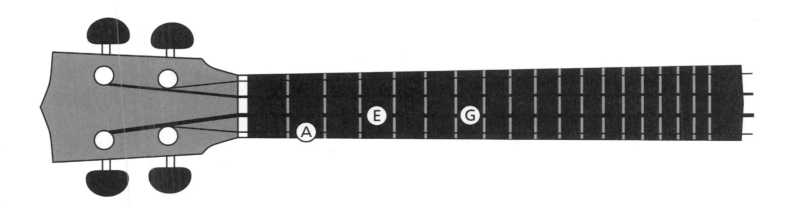

Electronic Tuners

Using an electronic tuner has lots of advantages: they're pretty fool-proof, and very precise.

Play the A string, and the device will show you on its display whether you're pitched too low or high.

Tune the string in the right direction and, when it's up to pitch, the display will let you know. Simply move on to the next string and so on, until the instrument is tuned.

PRACTICE

It's a good idea to get into a realistic practice routine right away. Practice is the key to improving on the ukulele, but it can also be the source of much frustration.

Here are a few tips to help you practise more effectively:

- A little practice every day is much more valuable than a finger-numbing mammoth session once a week.

- Keep a check on your posture and technique, to avoid any niggles creeping into your playing.

- Start slowly and build up: there will be a little wear and tear on your fingers to begin with, and it will take a bit of time to build up the calluses on your left fingertips—it's easy to overdo it, especially at the beginning.

- Set a target for each practice session, and make it realistic. Some people keep a practice diary, making a note of things to try in the next session. It's a great way to record your progress.

- Set aside time to play for fun. Keep it separate from your practice time, but make sure you sit and strum once in a while for no particular reason: after all, it's why you're learning to play ukulele!

Practising a little each day is the best way to build up your technique and confidence steadily.

READING CHORD DIAGRAMS

Uke players play chords, which are groups of notes strummed together, and are played using *chord shapes*. Chords are written down using chord diagrams, or chord *boxes*.

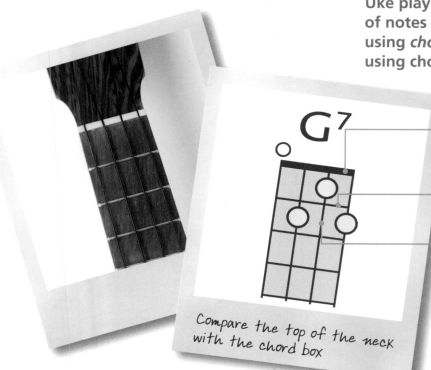

Compare the top of the neck with the chord box

Here's how they look:

The thicker line at the top is the nut—the white bone or hard plastic piece at the top of the ukulele neck.

The horizontal lines are frets—the wire divisions along the fingerboard.

The vertical lines are the strings, and the dots show where fingers are placed on the strings.

If an O appears above a string, the string is played 'open': without any fingers on it.

Here's how the chord boxes are used in this book—they are displayed upright, accompanied by a photograph of the fingers in a natural, horizontal position. Compare the diagram with the photograph to see how they relate.

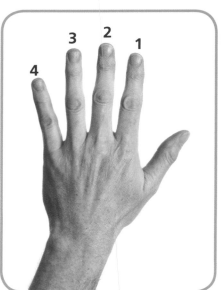

Uke players number their left-hand fingers like so.

LEFT-HANDER?

If you happen to be left-handed, there's nothing standing in your way to playing the ukulele. There's nothing specifically right- or left-handed about the uke, so they work either way around.

There are plenty of left-handed uke players out there, and as you work through this book, you'll simply need to swap the order of the strings around, and reverse every chord shape you see.

Now you're ready to get playing. So it's time to take a look at your first chords.

YOUR FIRST TWO CHORDS

To start playing songs, you only need to know two chords, so let's make a start with C and G7. Remember, the diagrams are shown upright, with the thick line at the top representing the nut—the piece at the top of the neck.

We'll begin by taking a close look at the way a single finger should sit on the fretboard. The fingertip should come down at right angles to the fretboard onto the string just behind the fretwire. If you find you're struggling to make a note sound without a huge effort, go back and check this basic finger position (see below).

Try placing the 3rd finger on the 3rd fret of the first string, like this:

The fourth, third and second strings are open, and the first string only is fretted. You're now fingering a C chord. If you brush down lightly across the strings with your right thumb, you'll hear the result.

All four strings should sound clearly. If the top string sounds a little muffled, or if the finger you're using on the top string is also touching another string, carefully adjust the position until you have the sound you're after.

Press the strings down as near as you can to the fret without them actually being on the fret. If you're pressing very hard to get a clear sound, there might be something a bit wrong with your finger position, so stop again and check that.

When fretting strings, aim to place the fingertip just behind the fretwire.

For now your right hand can simply curl up slightly and strum down across the strings. We'll get into some more advanced strumming soon, but for now just brush down with the thumb.

Brushing the strings with the thumb is a good way to hear how chords sound.

C is a *major* chord—it's a type of chord that often sounds bright and bold. Give the C chord another go, and once you're happy with it (and it doesn't have to be perfect for now) we'll move on to our second chord, the chord of G⁷.

G⁷ uses three fingers on three different strings, so it's more involved than C. Begin by placing the 1st finger on the 1st fret of the second string, and then place the 2nd and 3rd fingers either side, on the 2nd fret of the third and first strings. It might help to visualise the shape as a triangle. Here's how it looks:

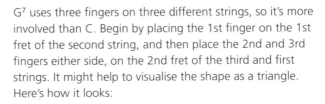

Visualising shapes is a great way to remember the finger positions. You'll soon see that many shapes have similarities to each other, and knowing what these similarities are will be helpful when it comes to changing from one chord shape to another in quick succession.

Now we'll take a look at a key skill: changing from one chord to another.

TOP TIP ✓

Changing from one chord shape to another is often more of a challenge than playing chord shapes on their own. Try to find any useful similarities between shapes to make the job easier.

CHORD CHANGES AND YOUR FIRST SONG

Take a look at this piece of music: it's four 'bars' long, and alternates between the chord of C and the chord of G7.

Play the exercise slowly through, and try to keep a steady beat.

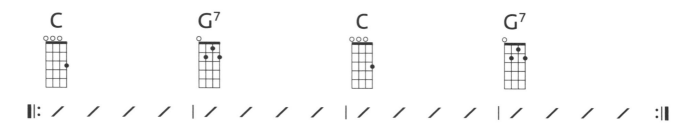

Strum down each time you see a slash (⟋). Each slash represents a single beat of music.

Four strums of C will make a *bar*, and then it's time to play a bar of G⁷.

The first few times, you might prefer to strum once on C, and count the four beats out while you change to G⁷. Try to play the G⁷ chord right at the beginning of the new bar.

Count again and change back to C, and so on. Once you have done it several times, you'll be able to strum slowly through, once on each beat without having to pause to change the shapes.

Notice the double bar lines with dots:

These are repeat marks, and are found either side of a repeated section of music. In this case, they indicate simply that the whole of the music should be played again.

When you're reasonably happy with the way things are going, you'll be ready to tackle your first song (opposite).

It uses both the chords you've just been playing, C and G⁷.

There are rhythm slashes as before, and this time arrows are added to show you to strum down at the beginning of each bar.

Later, when you can change between chords smoothly you could try strumming down on every beat, emphasising the first in each bar to help keep the rhythm going.

You don't need to read music notation to play the song on the next page: just follow the strums for the chords and sing the words.

If any of the songs in this book aren't familiar to you, listen to some recordings to learn the tune.

Try playing this gospel standard using the two chords. To start with, try just playing each chord once, clearly, at the beginning of the bar, and count through until it's time to play the next new chord. As you play, let your ears help you to tell which chord to play.

Soon you'll start to predict when the new chord comes by the sound it should make.

Take the song slowly, and try to move smoothly between chords. Check that your fingers are making the most efficient and accurate movements possible.

As for the right hand, again the movement should be smooth and steady. It's enough just to stroke the strings gently with the thumb.

Down by the Riverside

STARTING TO STRUM

Strumming is the most important technique to master on the ukulele, so it's worth looking at the basics before we go on and develop more advanced strumming styles.

Strumming involves playing across all four strings together in a rhythmic fashion.

In the previous song, we simply strummed down on the first beat of each bar. Now we're going to start stringing strums together to create rhythms.

DOWN-STRUM

Let's look first at strumming on every beat. The correct strumming technique for this is to brush down across the strings with the back of the index finger.

The hand should be held in front of the soundhole, with the other fingers tucked loosely in towards the palm, as shown. Use the wrist to create the movement, and brush gently across the strings in a single stroke. Try it using a C chord shape.

Once that's comfortable, and you're getting the sound you're after, try strumming this way in a regular fashion, counting "1, 2, 3, 4" out loud as you do so. Start slowly, and aim for an even, steady rhythm.

When the action's smooth, try playing at a slightly faster tempo (speed) but be sure to keep the beat steady.

C

1   2   3   4   1   2   3   4

Let's put this strumming into practice with the rest of 'Down By the Riverside'.

It uses a new chord, F, another major chord. The 1st finger is in the same position as for G⁷, with the 2nd finger on the 2nd fret of the bottom string:

Many people also play this chord with the 3rd finger on the 3rd fret of the top string (as it is for C), but you can leave the string open if you like:

Be sure to strum steadily down on every beat, taking special care to change from one chord to the next smoothly and swiftly.

Warm up with this simple exercise. It just alternates between C and F. You'll notice that the three-finger shape is shown for F, but feel free to use the two-finger shape if you prefer:

QUARTER NOTES

Up till now we've used simple rhythm slashes to show the count, but in standard rhythm notation a stem is added to the note head to show that the note lasts for a beat. This note value is called a quarter note (also known as a *crotchet* in the UK).

The stem can point up or down, depending which is tidiest in the music.

In strumming patterns where rhythm slashes are used, a stem is sometimes also added:

The quarter-note strums in the exercise at the bottom of this page have their stems added.

> Playing slowly is one of the most demanding performance skills—all the mistakes show up clearly and last for a long time! So be sure to iron out all the those little niggles before you pick up the tempo.

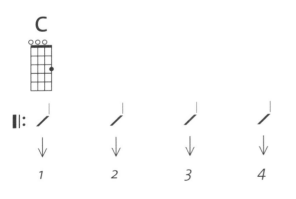

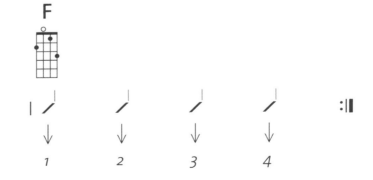

Down by the Riverside (complete)

Now that you know C, G7 and F, you can tackle the rest of 'Down by the Riverside'.

These three chords form the basis of hundreds of well-known songs.

Gon-na   lay down   my   bur - den,_   down by   the   ri-ver-side,_

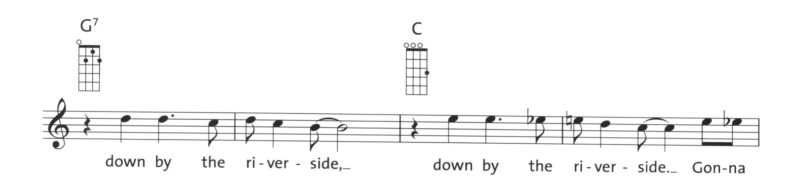

down by   the   ri - ver - side,_   down by   the   ri-ver - side._ Gon-na

lay down   my   bur - den,_   down by   the   ri - ver - side,_   and

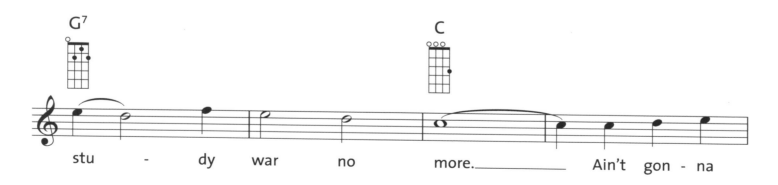

stu - dy   war   no   more._____ Ain't   gon - na

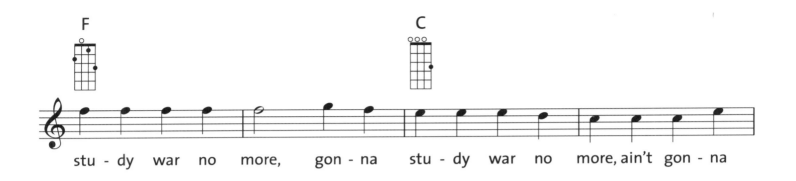

stu - dy war no more, gon - na stu - dy war no more, ain't gon - na

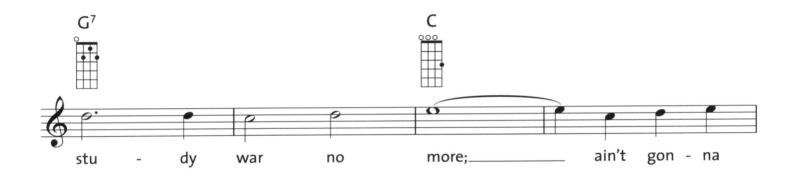

stu - dy war no more;_____ ain't gon - na

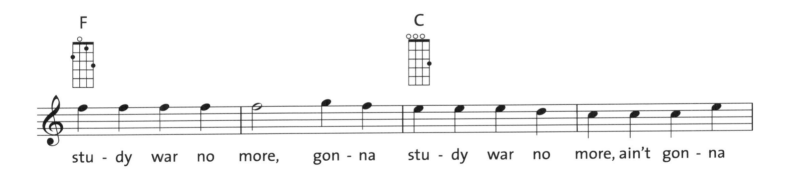

stu - dy war no more, gon - na stu - dy war no more, ain't gon - na

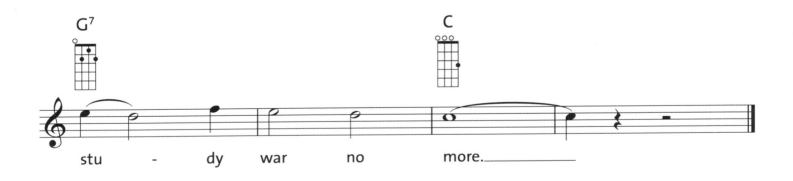

stu - dy war no more._____

UP-STRUM

Now let's think a little about what the hand does in between the down-strums.

Play through the exercises on pages 18 and 19 once more, and take a look at the right hand once it's strummed. You'll see, of course, that it moves back into position to begin the next strum. But when does it move? Just before the next strum? Right after the previous strum?

To play in the most relaxed, musical fashion, move the strumming hand back up right between the down-strums, exactly halfway through the beat. As you do so, brush the strings with the fingertip.

Here's how it would look. Notice how the 'in between' notes are counted.

The down strums are counted "1, 2, 3, 4" as before, but now there's an 'and'—shown with a + symbol—for the up-strums, too.

Count "1 and 2 and 3 and 4 and", strumming down, up, down, up, for a few bars, until you're comfortable with it.

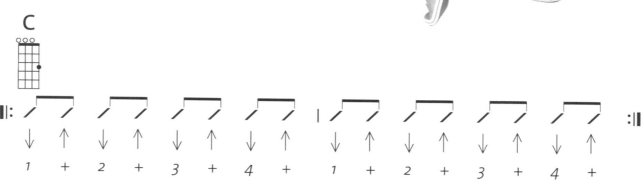

EIGHTH NOTES

In the exercise on page 22, there are eight strums in the bar, each worth half a beat. These notes are known as eighths (also called *quavers* in the UK), since there are 8 eighths in the bar. Where two eighths are played within one beat they are joined by a beam.

For strumming rhythms, the slashes now have tails and are joined in pairs indicating that each strum is worth half a beat (right).

Two eighth notes make a quarter note. Two eighths in one beat are joined by a beam.

NEW CHORDS

Let's take a look at another couple of chord shapes that crop up quite often in uke music. Firstly, C⁷, which is very simple to play: the first finger is placed on the 1st fret of the first string.

Also, here's D⁷. It uses the 2nd and 3rd fingers, on the 2nd fret of the fourth and second strings, respectively. These are both *seventh* chords, which are a special kind of major chord: you'll see a lot of them!

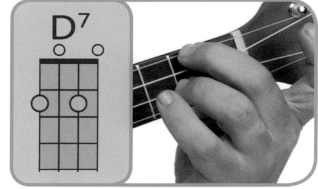

Now try putting these new shapes together with some you already know.

As before, this exercise changes to a new chord on the first beat of each bar.

Try playing quarter notes (down-strums only) or eighth notes (down- *and* up-strums). Once you feel comfortable, you could have a go and combining quarter- and eighth-note strums together—and even leave some strums out. In the next section we'll create strumming *patterns* this way.

 C G⁷ C C⁷

‖: / / / / | / / / / | / / / / | / / / / |

 F 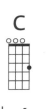 C D⁷ G⁷

| / / / / | / / / / | / / / / | / / / / :‖

STRUMMING PATTERNS

Combining up-strums and down-strums in a rhythm builds a strumming pattern.

Much of the energy in a song comes from the strumming pattern that accompanies it.

Patterns are often most effective if they're repeated throughout a section of a song.

Keep a note of strumming patterns that you like. You'll find that you use certain patterns over and over again. We're going to take a look at a very versatile pattern that is suitable for all sorts of songs.

Pretty much every strumming pattern we'll play using eighths requires the hand to strum down on the beat and up off the beat (between beats). Try the following pattern. it uses eighths, but not on every possible eighth note.

Sometimes the strums are allowed to ring on, which is indicated with the looped line joining notes together, known as a *tie*. Both bars contain the same rhythm:

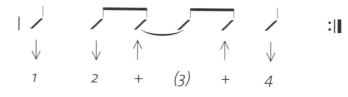

A tie is used to show that a note continues for the combined value of the connected notes.

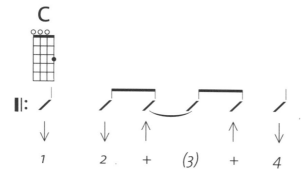

To help you, count "1, 2, 3, 4" as before, along with the 'and' if there's a strum at that point. You could also try clapping the rhythm before you play it on the uke.

Play the next song through with this pattern. Don't worry too much if you happen to 'catch' the strings when they ought to be silent—it'll simply give the music a bit more character!

Make sure that your strumming hand keeps moving down and up in eighths even if it's not making contact with the strings every time. This way you'll be able to keep the beat and play the pattern smoothly.

Careless Love

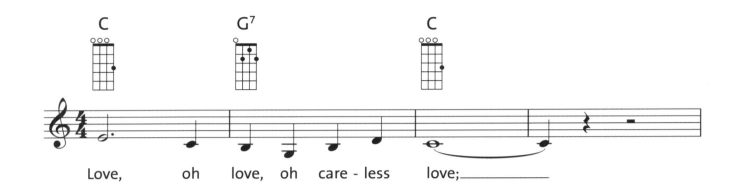

Love,   oh   love,   oh   care - less   love;_____

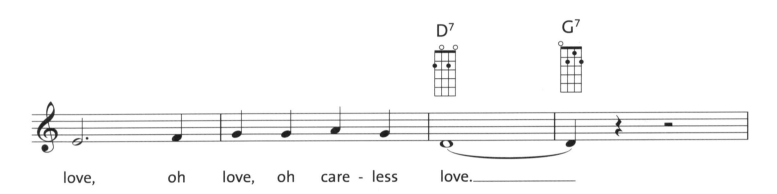

love,   oh   love,   oh   care - less   love._____

Love,   oh   love,   oh   care - less   love,   oh

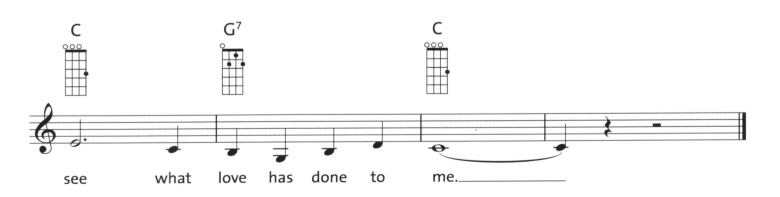

see   what   love   has   done   to   me._____

SWEPT STRUMMING

Now let's take look at a variation on the simple down-strum, known as a *swept* strum.

In essence the technique is just like a standard down-strum except that the strumming finger digs in a little to the strings, especially at the start of the stroke. As the stroke progresses, the movement is quite deliberate, sounding each string separately. This strum is indicated by a wiggly arrow.

Try strumming down across the strings in turn, just slowly enough that each string can be heard one after the other, like a ripple. Allow the chord to ring on after each strum.

We don't really think of standard strums as having a distinct duration—they just happen in an instant. But the swept strum takes longer: in fact, depending on how exaggerated it is, it can take long enough to 'eat into' the following beat, meaning the next strum will be late. The way around this is to *begin the swept strum early*: aim for the end of the swept strum to be right on the beat.

Try this rhythm, which should sound reminiscent of a tango beat, with four down-strums. The first strum is swept, with the other three played in the standard fashion. Be sure to start the swept strum early. Notice also the accent (>), indicating that the swept strum should be emphasised.

This time, the strum is staggered a little so that the individual strings are heard one after another as the strumming finger strokes them.

A wiggly line shows that the strum is swept. Strum across all the strings firmly but slower than usual, allowing each one to be heard separately.

C

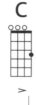     

1   2   3   4   1   2   3   4

This type of strum is especially effective combined with standard strums.

Let's build up a strumming pattern that combines various strumming techniques. Firstly, here's the pattern in its basic rhythmic form. The first two beats of the rhythm are identical to the pattern on page 24.

You'll notice there are two down-strums (*on* the beat) followed by three up-strums (*off* the beat). As before, try clapping the rhythm out while counting until you're happy with it:

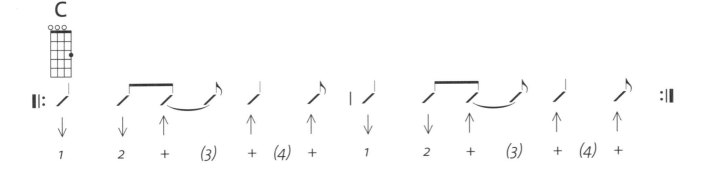

In the finished version, the 2nd beat is swept. You'll need to allow enough time to play the up-strum on the off-beat that follows, so make sure you begin the swept strumming during beat 1—maybe on the 'and', depending on how dramatic you want the strum to be.

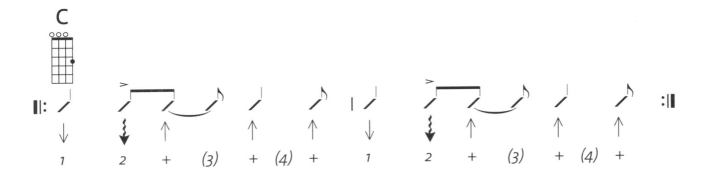

The swept strum is also accented, but the amount of emphasis is entirely up to you. Play around until you've got the timing and accent working as you want it to, and then use this rhythm to strum through 'Jamaica Farewell' on the next page.

Try this strumming pattern on any of the chords you've learnt so far, and practise it on the chord sequence from page 23.

Jamaica Farewell

Down the way___ where the nights are gay,___ and the

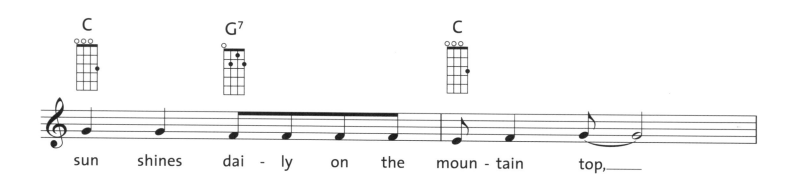

sun shines dai - ly on the moun - tain top,___

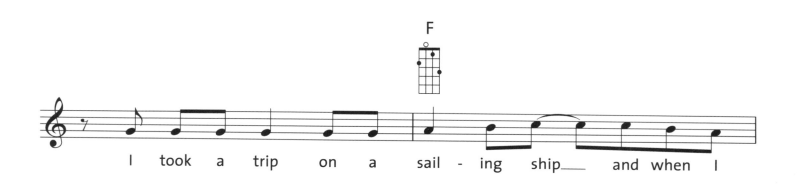

I took a trip on a sail - ing ship___ and when I

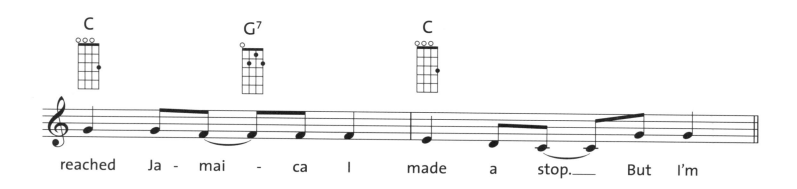

reached Ja - mai - ca I made a stop.___ But I'm

Remember: playing slowly is a difficult skill to master. Aim for a relaxed, steady feel for this song, with a strumming rhythm that brings out all the richness of the swept strum.

sad   to   say,____   I'm   on   my   way.____

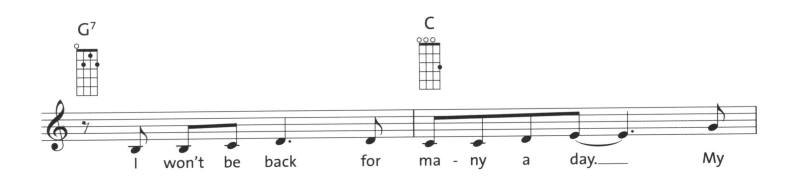

I   won't   be   back   for   ma - ny   a   day.____   My

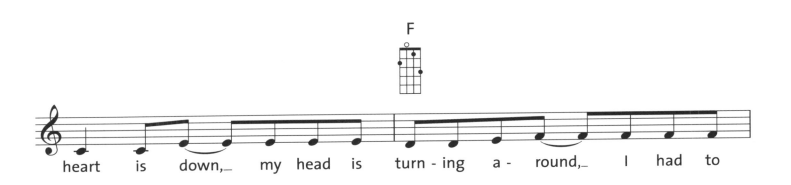

heart   is   down,_   my   head   is   turn - ing   a -   round,_   I   had   to

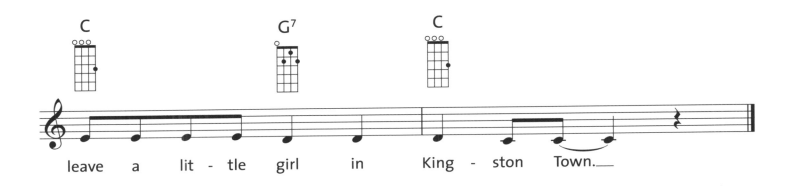

leave   a   lit - tle   girl   in   King - ston   Town._

READING TABLATURE

For strumming chords, diagrams showing left-hand finger positions are sufficient. But when it comes to finger picking, uke players use a more complete notation system. This is tablature, or *tab*.

Tablature is a musical notation system for stringed instruments that shows the performer exactly where to play each note on the fretboard. This notation is used instead of standard notation, which shows the actual pitches.

If you haven't yet learned to read either system, you should try learning tablature first. It's easier to learn, and it's especially useful for picking patterns.

The tablature system consists of four horizontal lines (a *staff*), each representing a ukulele string. The staff generally has a 'TAB' *clef* at the beginning of the staff.

The G string is the bottom line of the tablature staff, and the A string is the top line.

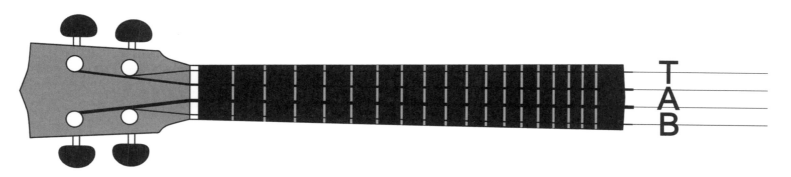

This layout is inverted from the actual string positions on the instrument. The string that in reality is closest to the ground is shown at the top, whereas the bottom line is shown uppermost.

A number on a line indicates at which fret to depress that string. This example shows various strings fretted or open (0).

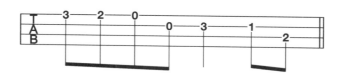

Sometimes, the stems and beams above or below the staff denote the rhythm. In this example, the rhythm is a combination of eighth notes and quarter notes.

FINGER PICKING

Instead of strumming chords, with all the strings played at the same time, uke players also pick the strings individually with the fingers and thumb. This is known as *finger picking*.

To pick the strings, use the nails or fingertips, depending on the sound you're after—and the strength of your nails!

The thumb plays the bottom string, with the index, ring and middle fingers playing the other three strings as shown. Some players like to place the little finger on the front of the uke to help keep the picking hand steady.

As with strumming, finger picking is played in patterns—repeated sequences. Tablature is ideal to show all the details for finger picking patterns.

Let's take a look at some fundamentals, and then we'll try picking on a well-known song.

TOP TIP

The trick is to play a picking pattern as a sequence, rather than thinking of the individual notes. This way it'll flow better and sound more natural.

Try this simple pattern, which again uses all four strings. In the fourth part of the pattern, the first and fourth strings are played simultaneously. The pattern then repeats.

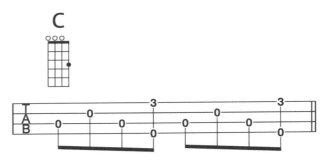

Take a look at the picking pattern below. It uses all four strings, as most patterns do, and with the shapes shown the notes of the chord are played in order of pitch, making it an ideal pattern for simple, unobtrusive accompaniment.

It's common to finger pick in eighth notes: two picks per beat. This creates an interesting texture without being too cluttered. If the tempo of the song is fast, however, it might be enough just to pick one note on every beat.

Experiment by accenting certain notes of the pattern. If you emphasise the *on* beats, you'll find the pattern sounds a little more solid—but overdo it and it'll become a bit too predictable. On the other hand, accenting some of the *off* beats can create *syncopation*, which will make the pattern sound more jazzy and lively.

In 'Banks of the Ohio' (overleaf) the pattern is made of four repeating eighth notes. Practise the pattern until it sounds smooth and relaxed.

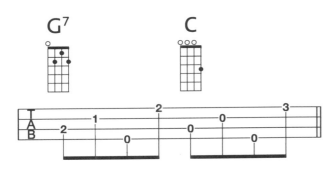

Banks of the Ohio

Now there are two lines of music to read at once! The standard notation is combined with the tab.

The picking pattern just repeats throughout the song, even when the chord changes.

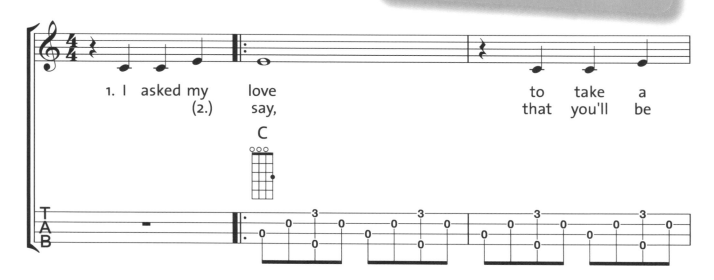

1. I asked my love
(2.) say,

C

to take a
that you'll be

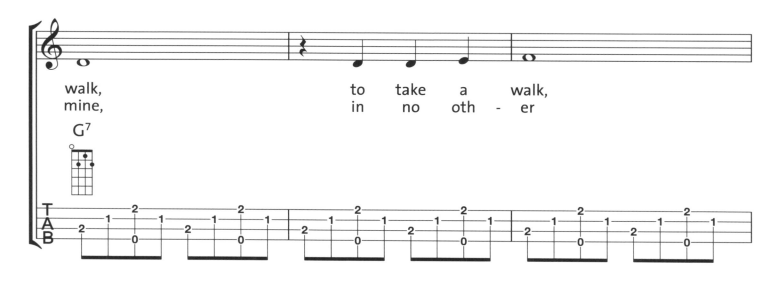

walk,
mine,

G⁷

to take a walk,
in no oth - er

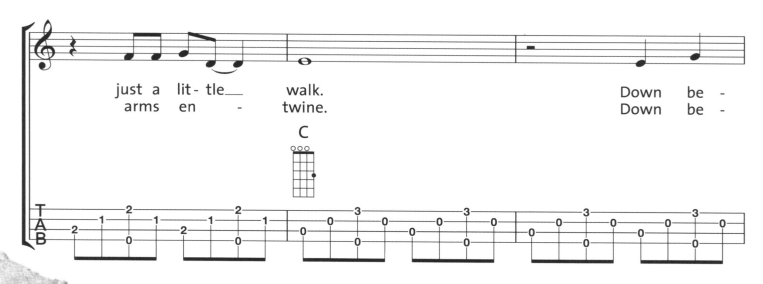

just a lit - tle___ walk.
arms en - twine.

C

Down be -
Down be -

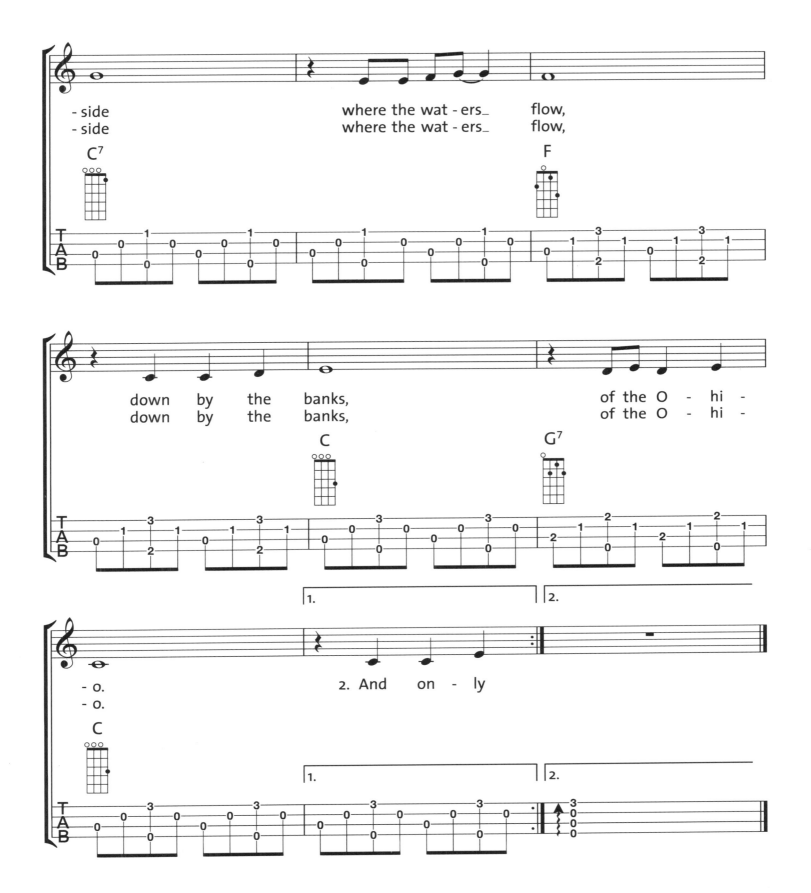

THE CHOP STRUM

Now that we've looked at some examples of strumming and picking, it's time to add variety to our accompaniment techniques.

The 'chop' is acheived by playing a heavy down-strum that is immediately *muted* (deadened).

Here's how it works. Play a down-strum with the back of the finger as normal, and at the end of the down-stroke bring the heel of the palm directly onto the strings. This will prevent the strings from ringing on creating a muting effect. A correctly 'chopped' strum will sound detached from those either side of it.

This detached sound is shown with a dot above or below a note. This is how it will look in a quarter note rhythm, with the chop on beats 2 and 4:

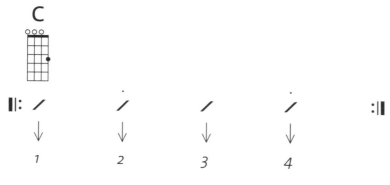

For the full effect, however, the chop should be heavily accented to provide a percussive element. It and can be followed by an up-strum just as if it were an ordinary down-strum.

Try this pattern in eighths, again with a chop on beats 2 and 4:

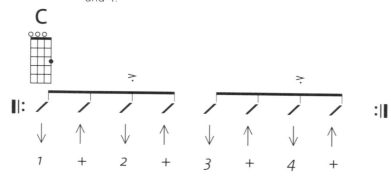

The chop strum is a variation of the down-strum that adds an accented, percussive quality to the strumming pattern. It's often used in up-tempo rhythms. Let's take a look at the basics, and then we'll fit it into a song.

SIXTEENTH NOTES

Some rhythms contains notes that last just half as long as an eighth note.

These are sixteenth notes, written with an extra flag on the stem. In the UK they are called *semiquavers*.

As with eighth notes, they can be joined together with beams. Four sixteenths make up a quarter note.

NEW CHORD

'Drunken Sailor' uses a new chord shape: Dm. The 'm' stands for *minor*, a type of chord that some people describe as having a darker or more sombre sound than the other type we've looked at, which are *major* chords.

'Drunken Sailor' only has 2 beats in the bar. Try strumming it through in sixteenths, with a chop on the '+'. It's just like the pattern on the bottom left, but played twice as fast.

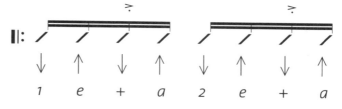

Notice the way the sixteenths are counted: "1 e + a 2 e + a" etc.

Drunken Sailor

PLAYING UP THE NECK

All the chords we've looked at so far have used at least one open string, and we haven't fretted any string higher than at the 3rd fret.

BAR CHORDS

The C shape we've been using so far has the top string fingered at the 3rd fret, with the other three strings played open. You could describe this shape as 0-0-0-3, which is how it would look in tablature:

Of course, the specific relationship between the notes on the various strings is what gives the chord its character. But you could easily play the same shape higher up the neck by use of a *barre*: a finger placed across all the strings to shorten the length of the neck temporarily.

Have a look at the shape below, in which every note is played two frets higher than the C shape. This means that the *relationship* between the notes is retained, so the character of the chord is the same, even though the *pitch* of the chord has been raised. Instead of a C chord, it's now D. The number of the lowest fret is shown in the diagram.

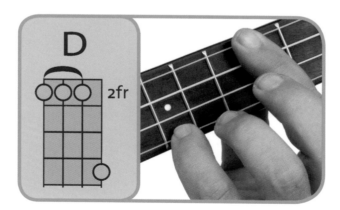

The chord of D, formed by playing a C shape played two frets higher. The barre takes care of the open strings and is shown in the chord diagram by a curved line across the barred frets.

Now it's time to take chord shapes to the next level. By making just a small adjustment to the shapes we've already come across, we can play them higher up the neck—dramatically expanding the range of chords we can play. It's time for *bar chords*.

The shapes in the song opposite are identical to those on pages 28 and 29, except that they are now played two frets higher. C is now played as D, F as G and G⁷ as A⁷. In fact for this version, *the 1st finger stays barring the 2nd fret for the entire song*. Turn to page 41 for an 'easier' G.

You can modify any standard shape by using a barre. Try playing the D⁷ shape, for example, barring at the 2nd fret. This way, instead of D⁷, you'll now be playing E⁷:

Sometimes you don't need a whole barre to modify the chord: a single fretted note will do. Below, Dm is raised two frets, and the 2nd fret on the top string is now also played, so it needs a change of fingering.

SHARPS AND FLATS

So how do you know exactly how far to move the shape up the neck? Here are some simple pointers:

● Chords and notes are named after the first seven letters of the alphabet, A–G. Going up the neck, there are two frets between any neighbouring letters. So E is two frets higher than D.

● This is always true except for two pairs: B–C and E–F, which are only one fret apart.

● To signify a note or chord raised by one fret, a *sharp* symbol is used (♯) as in C♯, G♯ etc.

● To signify a note or chord lowered by one fret, a *flat* symbol is used (♭) as in B♭, E♭ etc.

Jamaica Farewell (D)

Remember – barre the 2nd fret with the first finger throughout, and play the shapes just as you did on page 28!

Down the way_ where the nights are gay,_ and the sun shines dai-ly on the

moun-tain top,_ I took a trip on a sail-ing ship_ and when I

reached Ja - mai - ca I made a stop._ But I'm

sad to say,_ I'm on my way._ I won't be back for

ma-ny a day._ My heart is down, my head is turn-ing a - round, I had to

leave a lit - tle girl in King - ston Town._

TIME SIGNATURES

The songs in this book have so far had four beats in the bar or—in the case of 'Drunken Sailor'—just two. However, some songs have three beats in the bar.

There's no need to learn any new techniques for this new rhythm, but there's plenty of scope for new strumming patterns. First, however, let's take a look at the basics of counting the beats in the bar.

At the start of a piece of music you'll see a pair of numbers stacked one upon the other, somewhat like a fraction. Look at the song opposite: there's a 3 above a 4. This pair of numbers tells you about the number of beats in the bar, and is known as the *time signature*. Here's how it works:

The top number tells you how many beats there are in the bar; the bottom number tells you what kind of note is used to signify the beat.

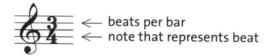

← beats per bar
← note that represents beat

All the songs we've played in this book have a '4' as the bottom number of the time signature. This means that a single beat is represented by a quarter note. The 2/4 time signature for 'Drunken Sailor', for example, has two quarter-note beats in each bar.

COMPOUND TIME

We're used to splitting beats into two: quarter-note beats subdivided into two eighth notes, for example. This is known as *simple time*.

But some rhythms split the beat into three. This is called *compound time*, and in such cases it's common to use 8 as the lower number. 6/8, for example, has two groups of three:

In 6/8, a pattern based on alternating down/up strumming would mean beat 2 is played on an up-strum. This is not especially easy to follow and can create an unsteady pulse. In the next section (page 40), we'll solve this issue.

Typically, three beats in the bar will create a 'boom-ching-ching' type of rhythm which is often heard in a waltz. The next song, 'Clementine', is an easy song that's ideal to try out *three-in-the-bar* strumming patterns.

COMMON TIME

4/4 is so prevalent in Western music that it's often referred to as *common time*. Sometimes, instead of the standard 4/4 time signature, a **c** is used instead:

STRUMMING IN 3/4

Here's a straightforward 3/4 pattern. The first beat is emphasised, with beats 2 and 3 being identical to one another:

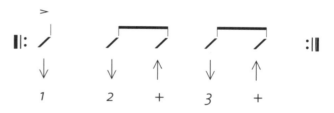

It might not seem especially interesting, but a simple accompanying rhythm is often all that's needed. It'll work perfectly well for 'Clementine', for example.

If you fancy something a little more involved, try this. It's essentially the same as the previous example, but this time it has a swept strum on the 2nd beat. Experiment with the precise timing of the swept strum until it sits comfortably in the strumming pattern.

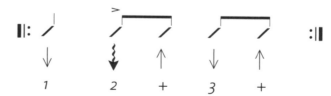

Try your own variations. 'Clementine' is such a simple song that you can add all sorts of strumming variations: perhaps changing the pattern for the 'Oh, my darling' chorus section, or maybe you could even devise a picking pattern that would work for the second verse.

Remember the old folk music saying: 'take it slow, keep it steady'.

Clementine

Notice the new chord, Bb. It uses a barre across the 1st fret on just the top two strings.

1. In a cav-ern, in a can-yon, ex-ca-vat-ing for a
(2.) was, and like a fair-y, and her shoes were num-ber

mine, dwelt a min-er, for-ty nin-er, and his
nine, her-ring box-es, with-out top-ses, san-dals

daugh-ter Clem-en-tine. } Oh, my dar-ling, oh, my
were for Clem-en-tine. }

dar-ling, oh, my dar-ling Clem-en-tine. You are lost and gone for

ev-er, dread-ful sor-ry, Clem-en-tine. 2. Light she

TRIPLE STROKE

Up till now, all the rhythms we've played have been based around alternating down-up strumming, since the beat splits into two.

The solution is to use the *triple stroke*. It's basically very simple, but takes a bit of effort to master. In the triple stroke, three separate strums are involved.

Strum down as normal with the index finger, but *leave the thumb* poised above the strings;

Strum down with the thumb;

Strum up as normal.

As we saw on page 38, some rhythms split the beat into three instead. This makes a simple alternate down-up movement awkward. Let's take a look at an option that allows us to play a natural, flowing strum where the beat is subdivided into three.

And here's how it's notated, with 'T' for the thumb stroke:

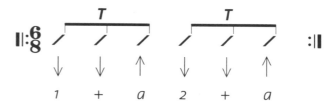

This pattern is also very useful for an up-tempo song in 3/4 time, where the beats are so fast that they're not split into two as they usually would be:

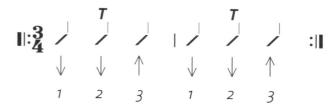

In the next tune, try the triple stroke throughout. Keep the beat steady—the natural 'boom-ching-ching' in the rhythm should help you.

The triple stroke is very handy for this kind of rhythm, and—as we'll see when we look at the *split stroke*—it has other uses too.

NEW CHORD SHAPES

There are a few new shapes here. The new G shape makes it easier to reach G⁷. You'll find yet another shape for G on page 43—they all have their merits and subtle differences in tone.

The D⁷ shape is played by barring a C⁷ shape on the 2nd fret (right):

The A⁷ is likewise a G⁷ shape raised by two frets (right):

Daisy Bell (Bicycle Made for Two)

DIMINISHED AND AUGMENTED CHORDS

Having played lots of major and minor chords, let's take a look at a couple of other types that often crop up in jazz-style tunes.

They're easy to play, and they'll extend your repertoire massively. They'll come in handy for anything from the blues to George Formby—and you can use them subtly in folk and rock too, just to give the music a bit more interest.

DIMINISHED CHORDS

The first chord type to try is the diminished chord. It's written as 'dim', or sometimes with a raised circle (°). It's played like so:

There's really only one sensible shape for the diminished chord on the uke, and it can be used up and down the neck depending on which exact chord you're after.

The shape is also interchangeable. Cdim is the same as Adim, F#dim and E♭dim, too!

> *Being interchangeable simply means that the diminished shape can be used for more than one chord.*
> *Cdim makes Ebdim, F#dim and Adim;*
> *Bdim covers Ddim, Fdim and Abdim;*
> *Bbdim works for Gdim, Edim and C#dim.*

In fact, this shape can be played *with* or *without* a barre. It amounts to the same thing. You might find it easiest to play with four separate fingers, or you might like to use the first finger to bar with:

AUGMENTED CHORDS

The other type to try is the augmented chord. It's written as 'aug', or sometimes with a plus sign (+), or as '#5'. There are a few different shapes you could play, all of which can be barred to play up the neck:

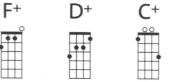

And, like diminished chords, they are interchangeable. F+ can be used for A+ and C+; F#+ for B♭+ and D+; G+ for B+ and E♭+; G#+ for C+ or E+.

Often, however, the augmented chord is used with a 7, written 7+. There are a couple of useful shapes for 7+, both using a barre. They looks like a mirror image of each other: As with the diminished chord shape, this one can be moved up and down the neck for whichever chord you need.

Here are some chord sequences that bring out the full flavour of the dim and ⁷+ chords.

The first one uses two diminished chords. Try playing them without a barre, and keep the little finger on the top string throughout.

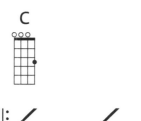

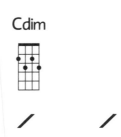

Compare the Dm⁷ shape with the Dm shape on page 36: just add your 4th finger on the 3rd fret of the top string.

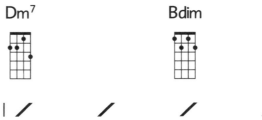

Here's a classic intro figure that would work on a song in G. This time, play the chords with a barre: the G shape is just a barred version of the first F shape on page 19. For the D⁷+, strum it once, letting it linger across the next beat.

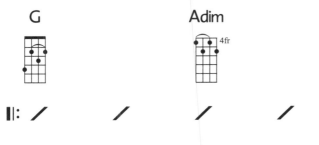

This is a typical use of the ⁷+ chord. Notice also the new shape for Am⁷: it'll come in useful in the next song. Notice also the G shape: it's simply a barred version of the first F shape on page 19.

And here's a four-bar phrase to get your teeth into, using a combination of various dim and ⁷+ shapes. Take a look at the G⁷ shape, too: it's a great moveable shape for ⁷ chords.

You'll certainly find it helps to memorise a chord sequence, especially when there's a bit more to it, as in this one. That way you can concentrate on the strumming.

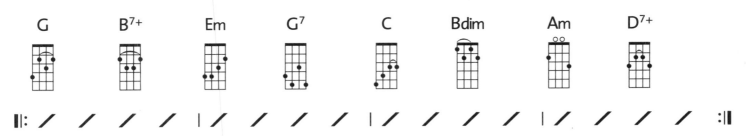

SWING STRUMMING

To give your strumming that authentic swing feel, which is great for the kind of sequence on this page, play in eighths as usual, but lengthen the down-strum and shorten the up-strum.

The idea is that the beat isn't strictly split into two equal eighths—instead, the down-strum is worth two-thirds of the beat, with the up-strum taking the remaining third. In practice, simply leaving the up-strum a little late will do the trick nicely.

The 'lilting' effect is more exaggerated at slower tempos.

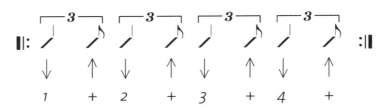

Split the beat unequally, with about two thirds of it going to the down-strum, to create an effective swing feel in your strumming.

SPLIT STROKE

The great George Formby pioneered a strumming technique known as the *split stroke*. The split stroke is at the heart of Formby's syncopated style.

It's an eighth-note pattern played over a four-beat bar, in which the natural movement of the strumming hand creates off-beat accents that give his trademark style its famous syncopated feel. It isn't difficult to understand, but it takes a bit of getting used to!

Let's go back to a simple eighth-note strumming pattern to start us off. The eighths are played in four groups of two (right). This is very steady, even and predictable, which isn't the case with the split stroke pattern.

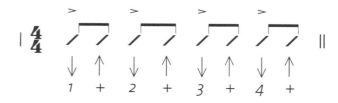

In the split stroke, the eighths divide up like this, with two groups of three, and a pair (right):

Try saying "Liv-er-pool New-cas-tle Lon-don" to get the feel of the 3+3+2 grouping. Say it a few times through without pause to get the feel. The off-beat accent on "New-" makes a syncopated rhythm.

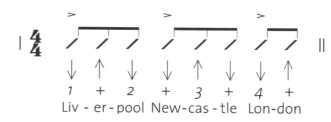

The only thing we really need to focus on is the first group of three strums. Here they are:

1. Strum down as normal across all the strings with the index finger: this is the accented note, so play a strong strum.

2. Now strum lightly up, just playing the top string or two. The main thing here is that the top string sounds clearly.

3. Finally, strum down, again lightly, on the bottom couple of strings only. This time the bottom string should sound out.

This group of three strums repeats, and the final two strums are steps 1 and 2 only. This is what it looks like in tab on a chord of C:

Play it through slowly until you really get a feel for the contrasting strums and the accents. Then try to get it as fast as you can!

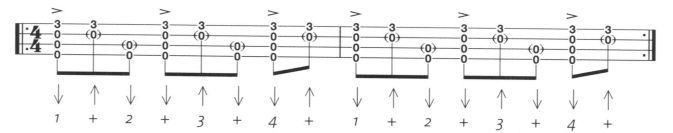

George Formby actually played a *banjolele*, which is a cross between a uke and a banjo. It has a loud, brittle sound, but the strumming works just the same on the ukulele. Now it's time to add the final details.

TAPPING

For the authentic Formby sound, it'll help to look more closely at the left hand. Typically, the finger that's fretting the top string stays on only for for the strong accents, being taken off for the others.

This is known in uke cirles as *tapping*. If the second and third strums of the group are played accurately, there will be a contrast between the fretted top string (**strum 1**), the open top string (**strum 2**) and the bottom string (**strum 3**)—the bottom string might be fretted or open, according to the chord shape. These notes combine to play a melody, clearly heard above the strumming rhythm.

Here it is with a bar each of C and G⁷:

DON'T FORGET!
The TOP string is nearest the floor, and the BOTTOM string is uppermost (see page 10).

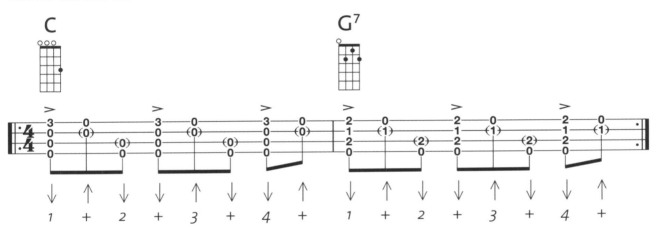

If you were feeling adventurous, you could occasionally add a triple stroke (page 40) on the 4th beat. In this case, you'll be fitting the three strums of the triple stroke into the beat.

Here, a triple stroke is inserted at the end of the first bar. Notice the square bracket and '3' on beat 4, indicating three strums played in the space of two.

Be sure to listen to some George Formby recordings to get the full flavour of his strumming style. The eighth notes are often lightly swung, and the accents are sometimes subtle.

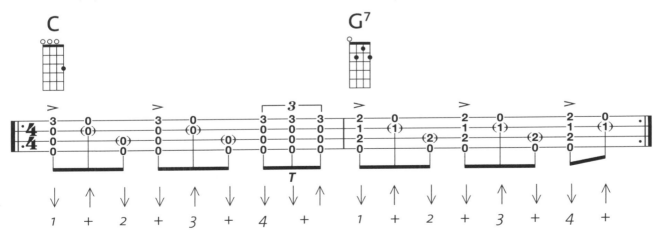

Bill Bailey

The opening four-chord sequence reappears at various points in the song, so spend a little time getting it 'under your fingers'. Once you can play it smoothly, you're nearly there. The rest of the song is in similar vein, with plenty of diminished and augmented chords.

The chord shapes are mainly variations of ones we've already seen, with a few useful new shapes—such as the Am7 in the intro, and the Am7 and Am6 shapes later on.

Once you've learnt the chord sequence, try adding split strokes and triples: the two bars of C on the second page would be a great place to branch out. Good luck!

GCEA

SOME USEFUL CHORD SHAPES

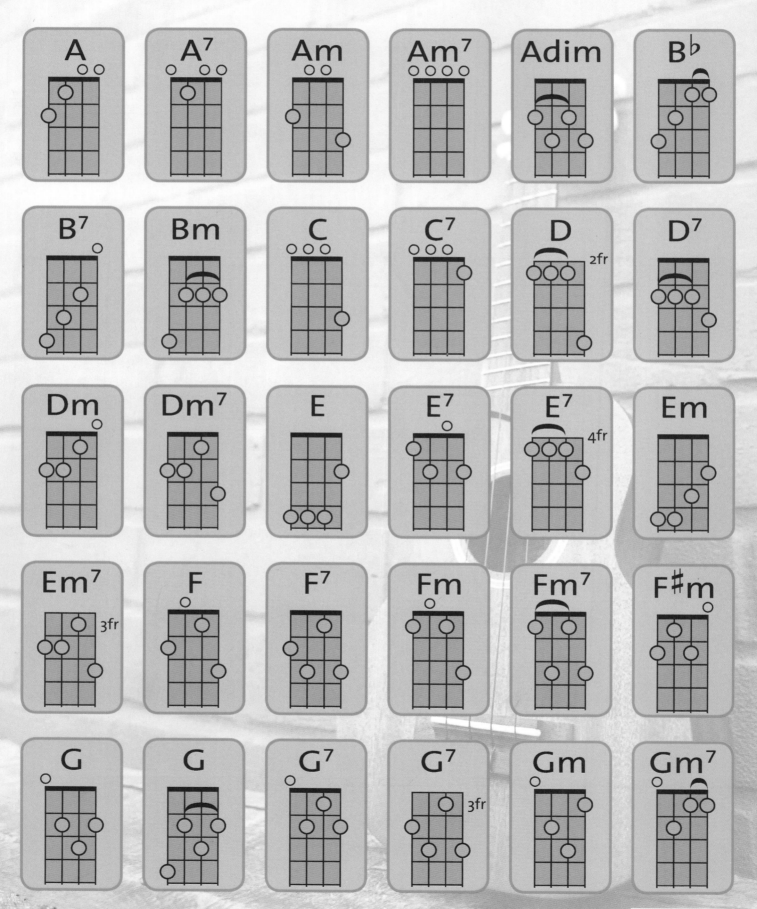

56789